The Friend Zone

This book focuses on a problem that of stuck in the Friend Zone. It talks about how to avo... you are there right now and how to get out.

Whilst this book is focussed on how to escalate and get physical with a girl, it also contains other tips and advice about dating including red flags, scams to watch out for and things to think about before taking things further and getting involved in a relationship or getting married.

How guys end up in the Friend Zone

When you meet a girl for the first time – at a bar, in class, in a social setting or at work, you probably think you need to be polite and friendly so that she likes you and doesn't get scared away. You really don't want to miss your chance with her so you play it safe, thinking that you first want to get to know her before you start to show your interest. So you become her friend first and before you know it, there you are in the friend zone, wondering how to take things to the next level.

Some guys stay in this situation for years, waiting for their chance or waiting for the perfect moment to tell the girl that they want to be more than just friends. The problem here is one of not knowing – does she like you or doesn't she? Well, if you never ask then you'll never find out and believe me, it's far better to know even if the answer is absolutely not because then you can move on. Later I'll explain how to find out of a girl likes you.

Another way that guys end up in the friend zone is when they approach a girl and try to get physical with her, but the girl turns them down and tells them they just want to be friends. This can be either because you made a major mistake in your approach or because she just doesn't like you. Sometimes a girl is interested at first and you go on dates with her but later she decides she doesn't like you and so she tries to let you down gently by saying "let's just be friends" or something to that effect. It can also be a way of breaking up.

The first type of Friend Zone situation could be better described as "not knowing" how the girl feels about you and the last two types are when the girl is "not interested". Obviously the solution to the first problem (not knowing if a girl is interested in you) is to find out if she is interested. I describe exactly how to do this below.

If the problem is that you're dealing with a girl that is not interested, then the solution is to accept this and stop dealing with her. Understanding this and accepting this fully actually makes it a lot easier because it helps you to lose any attachment you had to this girl and put the situation behind you. The problem is that for some guys this can be hard to accept because they have become attached to the idea of being with this person, so they keep trying and trying.

Refusing to accept this reality is like beating yourself over the head with a hammer - you keep thinking about her, wondering if she likes you etc. and then getting rejected again, and again... and again. By spending your time and your energy on a girl that has rejected you, you are just wasting time hurting yourself. If a girl rejects you, the best thing you can do for yourself is to accept it and move on.

Here's something that you should also be aware of. Some girls actually get a huge kick out of rejecting guys – this is how they get off. So rather than making it clear that they're not interested they send mixed signals. They get the guy to show his interest and then reject him. Then they make him think that they're interested again so that they can reject him again. They'll repeat this cycle over and over again as many times as they can because they enjoy it.

Why it sucks to be in the Friend Zone

When you really like a girl, every time you see her you imagine what you would like to do to her – how you would like to touch her, kiss her and be with her. The more you see her the more you like her, the more you imagine what it would be like to be with her and the more emotionally invested you become. If you hang around in this situation for a long time, sooner or later she will introduce you to her boyfriend or other men that she is interested in. If you're really deep in the friend zone she'll even start telling you all about her boyfriend and kissing him right in front of you. Eventually, when she finishes with her boyfriend you might think that your chance has finally come, only to see her up with someone else.

Avoiding the Friend Zone

Obviously the friend zone is a bad place to be – it's bad for you because it wastes your time, it's frustrating and it brings down your self esteem.

Some girls will dispute the fact that the friend zone even exists but if you've been there you know it's real. This is a good example of why not to take dating advice from women – women can't understand things that only men experience and they have very little sympathy anyway for men's problems. Women never experience this because men simply don't spend time with women that they find unattractive. If a man is not interested he makes this totally clear and doesn't want to hang out or spend time with a girl, so instead of being in the friend zone she just gets rejected. Or rather, he doesn't even approach her in the first place and, because women generally play a passive role, she therefore never even has to deal with a man that is not interested.

Women however, love to lead men on because getting attention from men makes them feel good (it makes them feel beautiful, valuable, sexy etc.). Some women really love this attention to the point that they'll go out of their way to make a man think she's interested just so that she can continue to get this attention. They'll do this by continuously sending messages, calling you etc but they never want to actually meet up or get physical with you.

Perhaps women don't like the term Friend Zone, but essentially it means being in a relationship that is not satisfying to you because you want more and the other person doesn't. It's not the same as actually being friends with a woman – this is a different matter entirely, but I think that it's only possible when you don't feel a lot of attraction for that woman.

Obviously you want to avoid the friend zone completely and if you ever find yourself in it, leave as quickly as possible. First I'll talk about how to avoid falling into it.

Firstly, don't spend time with a girl that you like without escalating. You have to be brave here and take the chance of getting rejected. Getting rejected isn't really bad thing if you think about it –it's actually a step up from "not knowing". It's better to know that a girl doesn't like you than spend a lot of time and energy on her whilst not knowing where you stand.

Getting rejected quickly is good because it means that you know where you stand can and can quickly move onto the next prospect. The quicker you do it the easier it will be because you will avoid getting attached or becoming "friends" with her. The longer you wait the harder it will be because those feelings will make it hard to move on. You really want to avoid developing feelings for someone that may not reciprocate at all. If you catch yourself doing this, stop. There are techniques for this – think about other girls that you like, make sure that you are talking to other girls, compare them with other women that you find more attractive, etc. But more than anything - find out quickly whether they like you back. Knowing that they don't like you from the beginning makes it really easy to let go.

Note that some girls will do everything they can to prevent you from finding out if she is interested or not by preventing your escalation in a very subtle way whilst still showing signs of interest. You need to notice this because this is a sign that she is leading you on deliberately and not really interested.

If you don't escalate at all, three things will happen:

1) It will be very difficult and awkward when you try to do it later because you will already have established yourself in her mind as a guy that doesn't escalate (it will seem out of character).

2) The girl will lose interest and start to think of you as just a friend.
3) Your feelings for the girl will grow as you become more attached to her and if she rejects you when you finally do get the courage to act it will hurt far more than if you had acted at the beginning.

Escalating means touching her physically. A girl that likes you will be receptive to your touch, whilst a girl that doesn't like you will not want you to touch her.

This is very important to understand. If you want to know if a girl likes you, touch her and see how she reacts. Don't ask her, because she may lie. Don't hint at something, because she may be (or play) stupid and not take the hint. If you touch her she faces a choice – either to let you continue or to stop you. She has to make that choice immediately and this will give you the information that you need.

Physical contact is what makes the difference between having a relationship and having nothing. It is essential. To do this you obviously first have to get a girl alone, so you need to create situations where the two of you can be alone together, otherwise other people will interfere and get in the way just by being there. Alone doesn't necessarily mean alone in a physical sense, but rather away from her friends or people that know the two of you. You don't want people watching you, especially the type of people that might comment or gossip about you. For example, a quiet corner of a bar is perfect because other people are minding their own business. A restaurant or café is not so good unless you find the perfect little corner, because it's hard to sit close together and you may have the waiter watching you or disturbing you every few minutes.

So in order to touch a girl first you have to get her into a situation where the two of you are alone together, away from her friends or other onlookers. If a girl makes an effort to avoid ever being alone with you need to notice this. It's not a coincidence. If she always brings along her friends to cockblock you or she avoids sitting or standing close enough to you that you could try to touch her, then you should take it as a sign that she is not interested. Women are not stupid – they know what they're doing. In fact, if a girl really likes you then she's likely to help things along by actually creating these situations and will readily agree or suggest going to some place where the two of you will be alone together.

Choosing to be in the friend zone

Once you know that a girl is not interested in ever getting physical with you, then you do have a choice. A girl can say "let's just be friends" but "let's" is just a proposal and therefore it's up to you whether you want to actually be friends with this girl. The "let's just be friends" really means "I don't want any physical contact with you, but if you want we can be friends as long as you never ever touch me".

It's worth thinking about this – sometimes you can have friendships with women that you were initially attracted to but that weren't interested. Sometimes these friendships can lead to meeting other girls the same age that you like even more, or can develop into genuine friendships. If you only had a weak level of interest anyway, then this can work. On the other hand, if this is a girl that you have a very strong level of desire for then that is going to be a problem because of the strong feelings that will keep coming up.

I actually have some great friendships with women that I used to be very attracted to and these friendships work because I no longer feel attraction for these women. Time passed and they lost their looks, put on weight or I just changed my type and started to be more interested in another kind of girl and so now I can hang out with these girls without feeling any desire to be with them. I don't care if they have a boyfriend because I don't want them. I have no interest now, so I deal with them if they're friendly on the same basis that I would deal with anyone else.

On the other hand, in the case of a girl that you really desire and that you can't stop thinking about – being her friend is a really bad idea. Every time you see her you will want her more and she will reject you again. Every time she sends you a message, you will hope that she has changed her mind and then be disappointed. If she tells you about other guys you will get pissed off and start comparing yourself to them. It's torture and it's not worth it, so don't do it to yourself.

Accept that this girl didn't want you and move on. The game is about finding the girls that want you, not trying to make things work with those that don't.

It might be a good idea, because of what I explained before, to avoid ending things on bad terms because with the passage of time a girl will eventually lose her looks and then you might actually want to be her friend. However, this can take a very long time (maybe 5-10 years?) and in the mean time you don't want to be in the friend zone. The priority has to be looking after yourself now rather than worrying about what might happen in 10 years' time.

When you tell a girl that you don't want to be her friend, some women can get quite arrogant and nasty or might try to lead you on and make you think that you still have a chance. They do this because they want to use you and take advantage of you or because they want to continue to enjoy the attention they are getting. Often they will insist on their offer of friendship and you have to turn that down with something like "don't call me again unless you change your mind". Make it clear that you don't want them hitting you up every day with "how are you, etc." just so that they can reject you again. Some women take a perverse pleasure in doing this – it makes them feel attractive and powerful, knowing that they can jerk your chain any time and you'll come running. In a way they are like energy vampires, sucking away your energy and confidence so that they can boost their own.

Some girls will talk with you all day long, but nothing will ever happen. You need to put them in a position where they have to make a decision and the consequences of that decision are either something happens between you or you stop seeing them. There should be no middle ground. Otherwise you are giving a woman the space to play with you and some women will take that and run with it. In fact, some women have a whole "team" of guys that they are doing this to. Of course, when they hit the wall at 30-35 the whole team drops off and nobody wants them, but that's for another book.

It is extremely unlikely that any girl that has put you in the "friend zone" will ever be more than friends with you because of the reason that she put you there in the first place: she simply doesn't find you attractive. Maybe she's too polite to tell you and she may give you all kinds of excuses (I'm not looking for a relationship right now, you're too good for me etc.), but that's the cold hard truth. Don't waste time pining after a girl that already had a chance to be with you and turned you down. Instead, find out quickly whether they are down and then boot them out of your life forever if they are not (or at least cut them off until they hit the wall and then they can be your friend, knowing that you no longer feel any desire for them).

Getting Out of the Friend Zone

If you are in Friend Zone A (you haven't shown a girl your interest yet) then it might be possible to get out. Obviously, the way to do it is to start escalating (getting physical) with her and see what happens. If she lets you continue and you end up kissing or having sex, then you're out of the Friend Zone. However, if she stops you (and I don't mean just slows you down but stops you completely because she doesn't want any physical contact) or she says "let's just be friends" then you're in Friend Zone B.

You can never get out of Friend Zone B. The reason for this is because of the reason you are there the first place: the girl wants you to be "just a friend" because she doesn't find you attractive. Friend Zone B is where a girl puts guys she has ruled out as boyfriend material. Whatever the reason for that is, she is likely to keep it to herself.

However, she is highly likely to be telling her friends exactly what it is about you she doesn't like and perhaps even bragging about it. If you really want to find that out, you could try asking common friends what she has said about you or you could find a more sneaky way of finding out (but don't use spy software or pretend to be someone else because that would be wrong). You could also try making her really angry and then she might tell you straight out (because then she wants to hurt your feelings rather than protect them or avoid a difficult moment).

Whilst knowing the truth might be helpful so that you can improve your weak points and get over her, the most important thing is to accept that she's not interested and not waste time trying to get with a girl that has already ruled you out. If necessary, cut all contact and don't see her anymore. There is only one 100% guaranteed way get out of the friend zone – by not being friends with her anymore.

The Nuclear option

Some women can be really, really insistent that they want to be your friend. They won't go away, because secretly they love the positive feelings they get from knowing that you want them and so they keep on feeding you crumbs to keep you on the hook. After making them put up or shut up, i.e. finding out if they are really interested or not, as described below, once you've established that they're not interested you really need to get rid of them and stop them from coming back because otherwise they will keep coming back, lapping up the attention and then rejecting you again. This cycle can repeat indefinitely and you need to break it. You need to kick these women out of your life forever, and kick them so hard and so far that they will never want to come back. This is what I call the nuclear option.

Obviously, I mean this metaphorically and not literally. You shouldn't actually kick anyone. What I mean is you need to say something really offensive or rude or whatever it takes to get rid of this person forever. Stop being polite, stop holding back and let them have it. Of course, they'll probably come back at you with a bunch of insults but curiously this can actually be a good thing. It's quite likely that, in their rage, they'll tell you exactly what they think of you (i.e. how unattractive they think you are) and they'll even give you specifics (you're too fat, too ugly, not their type or whatever) that they would never have revealed if you had asked them. If you make them really angry, girls will often blurt out the truth that they've been hiding all along. This is good because it will 1) Make it really easy to get over them. 2) Make it impossible for them to ever trick you again into thinking that they like you. 3) Make them stop wanting to come and feed off you for compliments and favours, because they know that you could blow up at them again at any time.

The nuclear option. Try it, folks!

Finding out if a girl likes you

You can't make a girl like you, but what you can do is quickly find out if she likes you and choose not to be friends with her if she doesn't. It is important to do this as quickly as possible so that you don't start to get feelings for her and if she turns you down then you can not feel hurt and quickly move on. I would advise not being friends with a girl that you really want to be more than friends with, for the reasons I talked about above. However, if you think her friendship is worth keeping (and you won't feel bad about never being with her or seeing her with other guys) then you can stay her friend. Another option is just to cut or reduce contact for a while to give you the chance to meet someone else that you like more than her. Some girls seem to think that they can just declare "you're my friend" and that makes you their friend whether you like it or not. The best way to deal with this is to just never speak to them again.

So, the key is to find out **quickly** if a girl likes you. Now I will talk about how to do that..

Asking

This might seem like a scary thing to do but it will save you a lot of time and frustration. Once you know a girl doesn't like you are not going to waste time doing her favours, hanging out with her or trying to impress her etc, which really is completely pointless if the girl doesn't even find you attractive. However, you should be cautious about how you ask because often girls will try to avoid telling you outright that they don't find you attractive for several reasons:

- They want to avoid an awkward scene
- They don't want to hurt your feelings
- They don't want to have to explain why they don't like you
- They like being complemented and having favours done for them etc

- They want you to be their friend and don't want to lose you (in that boring platonic sense)
- They are trying to take advantage of you

Although it is true that it's generally a bad idea to just ask a girl if she likes you, it's better than doing nothing and just waiting and hoping. Anything is better than that. Rather than asking this question with words, the best way is to do it subtly and use physical escalation as I will explain below. If you do have to ask with words, take into account that a lot of girls will try to avoid actually answering by ignoring you, changing the subject or pretending not to understand. Then, when they do answer they might lie. With physical escalation they don't have any of those options and their response is far more likely to be a truthful response (it's hard to fake).

Excuses

One key thing to understand with women is that they'll often avoid saying anything directly. They really don't like directness, in general. So if you ask a girl if she likes you, she will often just ignore your question or pretend not to understand. Only if she really likes you a lot will she respond to these types of questions. Essentially, a girl will do anything to avoid actually having to say "no". They want you to understand that the answer is no without having to say it. If the answer is yes, they will show it to you and they also expect you to get the message without having to say it. This is because girls also don't want to have to deal with rejection.

Escalation

If you are interested in a girl, it's best that you make that clear through your actions (not words) as quickly as possible. Don't hang around as a friend and then suddenly surprise her with some kind of "declaration of love" or anything like that. Instead, escalate physically from the first time you meet her (meaning get close to her and touch her more and more until it eventually leads to kissing and having sex). Do it step by step, but do it quickly.

By quickly I mean that you should start as soon as you meet a girl for the first time. By step by step I mean that you should not touch a girl you don't know in an intimate way or try to kiss her. You can eventually get to that but you need to touch her in other less threatening ways first and get her unspoken consent before going further.

Of course, if you live in a "yes means yes" state then you should probably get some contracts drawn up by a lawyer and get her to sign a consent form in front of 5 witnesses before you even touch her on the knee. Otherwise, in general, you should absolutely not ask for "permission" because most women will automatically reply no and it kills the vibe. Women don't want you to ask them for permission before touching them, whatever the crazy hardcore feminists and professional victims say. It turns women off and if you don't believe me just try it. It makes you look weak and inexperienced and that makes women lose respect and attraction for you.

Anyway, what you do need to do is get the girl used to being touched by you and comfortable with it before you progress further, so you need slowly increase contact so that she can imagine where it's going next and feel that she has control over the situation. She needs to know that she can stop you at any time, but that if she doesn't you will continue and take it further. Back off if she appears uncomfortable, but don't give up completely. Just go back to the previous level of contact that she was comfortable with and then gradually increase it again.

To start, you need to create a situation where you will both be alone somewhere and then sit as close as possible, ideally so close that you are touching. Then, just lightly touch her on the arm or shoulders as you are talking. This should not be difficult because it is quite normal to touch a person that you are talking to. Without noticing you probably do it all the time with your friends or people you meet. So the first time you touch a girl she should feel that you touched her, but not think anything of it. However, she will show some kind of reaction and either move in closer or move away. You need to notice how she reacts.

What you need to do is be very subtle and very gradually increase the amount of touching. If at any point you move too fast you are likely to get a negative reaction and things will become awkward. You also need to be very alert to how the girl is reacting and notice how she responds. If she is smiling, looking at you in the eyes and not moving away then you can gradually increase the level of touch and see if her reaction changes.

Once she gets used to you touching her occasionally on the arm or the shoulder as you talk, or perhaps putting your arm on her back as you walk along together, you can go to the next level, where you leave your hand there for a few seconds. Again, watch her reaction very carefully. She could pull away or stay there. She might also start to touch you back.

The reason that touch is much better than words is because people can lie. People lie for many reasons: they may not want to hurt your feelings, they may want to manipulate you into doing favours for them, they may just be shy or want to avoid the awkwardness of turning you down... But it's almost impossible to lie with your body. Some clues will always be there. If you pay attention and know what signs to look for, you can see very clearly whether a girl likes you.

Before I continue, think about this just to get an idea of how it feels from the other side, being the girl: how would you feel if someone that you weren't at all attracted to sat too close to you. You would move away, right? Now imagine that a beautiful girl sat close to you. Would you move away? Obviously not, you would stay and enjoy it. You would probably smile at her and start feeling turned on. What about if her hand brushed against yours? Would you move your hand away? Probably not - you would enjoy it and want to keep your hand there as long as possible. At this point you would both notice that there was a mutual attraction as you would effectively be deliberately touching each other. The first time this happened to me I knew for sure that the girl I was with liked me – and this was a girl that that I was meeting at a café for the first time to give her an English lesson. The next time she called me the lesson was in her bedroom… (I know that sounds like a corny joke but it actually was, and because of the way our hands had touched before I felt there was something between us so I made my move and we ended up kissing).

Of course, you can't just wait for the girl to make a move like this. Girls sometimes do if they really like you, but unfortunately it is normally the man that that is expected to make a move and women play a very passive role. If you don't do it, girls will quickly forget about you and assume that either you were not interested or do not have the confidence to make a move, which makes you look weak and therefore less attractive. Also, you have to understand that any pretty girl won't be available for long. If you don't make a move on her when you get the chance, you may never get the chance again, because she'll quickly get snapped up by someone that moves quicker than you.

Now here is the important part in all of this. Any time you touch a girl in any way: see what happens. Watch the girl's reaction very carefully. She *will* react in some way. It is physically impossible for her not to. And if you're paying attention, this reaction will tell you clearly whether or not she is interested.

Firstly, and obviously, she could react negatively. There are several ways she could do this. She could ask you why you are touching her, but this is unlikely unless you move too fast or overdo it in some way because it creates an awkward scene and most girls want to avoid that. Some women are disagreeable by nature though and take pleasure in creating awkward scenes and drawing attention to themselves. If that's the case you have two reasons not to pursue her any further. She could move away from you or put some kind of obstacle between you or her (for example by sitting on the other side of a wide table or placing her bag or purse between you). She could also find some excuse to leave or start paying attention to her phone or someone else, or even invite other people to come over so that they can cockblock you by getting in the way and making it impossible to be close to her. In most cases she is likely to be quite subtle, but if you are paying attention you will notice what she does.

Basically, anything she does that makes it more difficult for you to continue escalating should be considered negative. Putting her handbag in the space between you, sitting across from you, leaning away… In this case you should slow down and even stop completely if the signs are clear. Don't keep trying to touch a girl that is showing she's uncomfortable and doesn't want to be touched. This will only get you into trouble or lead to an awkward scene because she will have to make it more obvious so that you understand. If a girl's reaction is negative, it's best that you give up on her and look for someone else. The sooner you realise this the less time you will waste, which is why you should try to move as quickly as possible so that you know the situation before you get emotionally involved.

Secondly, she could react positively. This may be very subtle but it will be obvious if you are paying attention. If she moves closer or touches you back in any way then this is a positive reaction.

The important thing is to increase gradually, not suddenly. If you are sitting close, with your arm around her and holding hands then a kiss at this point is the next logical step. But make it a small kiss. If you suddenly try to jam your tongue down her throat you'll "break the spell" and make her feel that you're unpredictable or too pushy and that she's not in control.

By increasing the level of touch gradually I don't necessarily mean slowly. It is possible to go from casually touching a girls arm for the first time to having sex with her within a very short period of time, but the point is that you have to pay attention to how she reacts to your touch and give her the chance to stop you if she wants before you try taking it any further.

The third way she could react is neutral. She doesn't move away or try to stop you from touching her, but she doesn't do anything to encourage you like touching you back or moving closer either. This is the actually most common reaction and it is not really a bad thing –if she doesn't move away (as long as she is easily able to do so if she wants) then by not moving she is letting you touch her.

The good news is that this is a not a red light but more of an amber. It more or less means "proceed with caution". Girls know that as soon as they start touching you back this gives you a green light to take it further so they may prefer to just let you continue what you are doing and enjoy it. To understand this you have to think about it this way: imagine you were the one being touched. By staying where you are you would be allowing it to continue. If you want someone to stop touching you, you move away. Of course, you need to be careful in the sense that you need to make it clear that the girl is free to go at any time. Don't put a girl in a situation where she could feel trapped or coerced.

With a neutral or a totally passive reaction, you have to go very slowly and be careful, especially if you are dealing with a girl that is extremely shy, nervous or intimidated by you for whatever reason, such as an employee or someone that you have authority over. But between equals, lacking any potential feeling of "obligation", if they are sitting close to you and letting you touch them then it is probably because they want to. However, you have to look for other signals. Do they look excited or uncomfortable? Are they looking around for an excuse to escape? Give them a chance to move away if they want. Otherwise continue, but only increase the level of touching very slowly.

You should understand all of his as a sort of green/amber/red light from the girl. Sometimes the girl will switch between amber, green and red, sometimes responding, sometimes being passive and sometimes moving away or stopping you from moving things forward to the next level. What is important is that you understand these signals and obey them. Stop when she wants to you to stop, be cautious when her signals are unclear and keep moving things forward when she gives you a green light. This will make her feel comfortable because it shows you know how to lead and take things forward but that you will slow down or stop any time she wants.

Sometimes a girl will give you amber (passive) signals until at some point she suddenly "let's go" and starts kissing you passionately. Sometimes she will give you green or amber signals and then at some point give you a hard red (normally this happens if you try some kind of unexpected sudden move or you come up against a limit in her mind as to how far she wants to go).

Understanding this makes it quite easy to gauge a girl's interest level quickly and efficiently, even if she tries to hide it from you. For example, if a girl wants you to think she's interested so that she can take advantage of you or get favours from you she might contact you often, smile at you and keep giving you little crumbs of hope, but whenever you try to escalate on her she'll give you a red light because she's not really interested. And she has to give it to you because the only alternative is to let you keep on going, getting more and more intimate, so at some point she'll have to stop you if it's not what she wants.

Levels of intimacy:

1. Friendly touching: touching a girls hands, shoulder or arm in a casual and non-prolonged way as you might do with a friend. It doesn't necessarily mean anything (but she can still feel it and if she likes it she'll move closer). At this stage you should only touch her for a second or two at the most.
2. Affectionate touching: touching a girl affectionately – putting your arm around her shoulders or waist or touching her hands, shoulders or legs in a more obvious or deliberate way. At this point the girl knows that you are touching her because you like her. You might put your hand on her arm, but keep it there for a few seconds. She will notice the difference and again, it's up to her if she moves her arm away. She becomes aware that if she lets you, you are going to keep touching her so she has a choice – to stay or to move away, but she knows where it will lead if she stays.
3. Sexual touching: after you have been touching a girl in an affectionate way for a while, you can start to become a bit more daring and move your hand slowly to explore other parts of her body. If you have had your arm around her waist for a while, you could move down a bit towards her bum or from her legs you could go to her stomach (missing out the bit in between for now). By this point you could probably go for the kiss if you haven't already. After kissing, your hands

can start to wander more but if she stops you just go back to the stage before and leave that for later whilst you touch her somewhere else. Eventually you will be touching her inside her underwear and I don't really need to tell you what happens next....

The important thing is to always go step by step. You can't just touch a girl in a place where she is not expecting it, but if you are already touching a girl on the stomach and kissing her neck she could reasonably expect your hands to explore a bit further. Just keep watching her reaction as you do this and slow down/stop based on the signals she gives you. Sometimes she may make you stop at a certain point. In this case don't give up hope, but stop for a while and then later try again to take it to the next level, but always go one step at a time so that she has the chance to stop you if she wants. That will make her feel comfortable (because she can stop you anytime) but also excited because she knows there's a certain danger with you (if she doesn't stop you, then it is inevitable that this will lead to sex). To give another analogy –keep on the accelerator but make sure she knows that she controls the brake.

How Not to Escalate

Kevin Spacey is currently going through a bad time in the media because of something that allegedly happened 30 years ago. I don't know whether it is true, but story is that he was coming on to a guy and he did what I recommend not doing – he made a sudden and unexpected move, involving grabbing a guy and getting on top of him.

I don't know about coming on to guys because that's not my thing, but I have had the unfortunate experience of guys trying to come on to me and it gave me a taste of what women feel when they don't like the person that is trying to touch them. If it happens subtly and slowly then you can easily stop it before it becomes a problem, but if they make a sudden move you don't have time to react and, if they go too far, could legitimately feel violated. One thing is someone sitting too close or brushing their hand against yours (in which case you can just move away and they will get the message) and another thing is them suddenly trying to grab your dick or kiss you on the mouth.

This is why I always say: don't make any sudden moves. Doing this is likely to get you into trouble or scare the girl away. You have to increase the level of physical contact gradually and watch how the girl reacts. If she reacts negatively you have to back off. If you ignore a girl's signals and keep going when she wants you to stop, then you're going to mess things up.

Go through the all other stages first – touch her lightly on the hands, her arms and other less sensitive parts of her body and do it in a casual way at first and only gradually get more obvious when she responds or shows that she's ok with it. This will take as long as it takes depending on how the girl responds, but if a girl really likes you it won't take long at all. Sometimes you can go from the first touch to sex very quickly because the moment you start touching her she'll start touching you back or you will see that she's getting turned on and it will just happen. There is no need to ever suddenly just lunge at someone. Imagine how you'd feel if some person you find unattractive did that to you.

Another analogy is getting into a hot bath – do you just jump straight into the steaming hot water or do you put a toe in first? You need to test the water first before you jump in. On many occasions I've found it very useful to be able to find out if a girl was into me and you can do this in front of other people (her friends, your friends, other guys that are interested in her etc) without anyone even noticing. It's so subtle sometimes even the girl doesn't consciously notice what you're doing – she just feels turned on and realises that something could happen between you if she lets it happen. Don't expect girls to take much of an active role –this rarely ever happens.

Again, don't make any sudden moves, by which I mean suddenly increasing from a light touch on the arm to touching her breasts or trying to kiss her. For example, before touching her breasts you need to have touched her legs, stomach, hands, shoulders, neck etc and have kissed passionately and you need to touch close to that area first to test the water and see if there is any resistance. If there is just move away again and touch her where she is comfortable. Don't force her to shut you down completely, because if you do then it will probably put an end to everything because you made her feel uncomfortable.

If a girl shuts down your attempts to be more than friends, then it is up to you whether you still want to be friends with her. Personally, I think it depends how strong my feelings are about a girl. I can be friends with a girl that I didn't really want that much anyway, but I can't be friends with a girl that I really like. There can be advantages to staying friends, as long as you are able to accept that is all there is and will ever be. But if you can't accept it, it best to stop seeing this person.

General Advice about New Relationships

Anyone that has experience with women will also know that sometimes you can meet the most beautiful girl and think that you are the luckiest guy in the world, but later she turns out to be an absolute nightmare. When you are overwhelmed with the good feelings that come from a new relationship you might not be able to think critically so I also talk about some red flags to look out for and how to slow things down so that you don't find yourself in too deep when you realise you need to get out.

Knowing what you want in life

What is it that you want in life? Do you even really know? Maybe you think that you what you want is to meet lots of beautiful women and have lots of sex. Lots of men believe this. But once you get a beautiful girl that you are crazy about, would you really want to leave her and be alone again just so that you can go to look for others? Maybe you don't know the answer to that yet because you have never had to make that choice, but it is something to think about.

If you are starting out on this journey, especially if you are young or inexperienced, you might be thinking the opposite: if I could only find one beautiful girl that liked me I'd be happy forever. This is also an illusion, as you will find out if you don't know already. Beauty doesn't last forever, and even if it did no one person can ever solve all of your problems or be everything you want. In fact, they may bring you new problems that you didn't have before, perhaps serious ones.

If you are thinking like this then the first thing you have to do is come back down to earth and be more realistic. Getting into a relationship may be something that you desperately want, but getting into a bad relationship can be very damaging so you should proceed carefully. You also shouldn't focus so much on this area of your life that you neglect everything else. Don't forget who you are and what you want in life just to please someone else and keep a relationship going, or you will end feeling lost and wondering what happened to your life.

Being lonely

Being alone can be seen as a bad thing but is it really? There are advantages to being alone: you can do whatever you want, go wherever you want, speak to whoever you want, spend your money on whatever you want. Nobody is looking at your messages, getting jealous or angry, complaining, nagging or telling you what to do. You are not loaded down with responsibilities. If a new job or travel opportunity comes up, you can take it. You can decide at any moment to move house, move to a different country, change your career, or even go back to school because nobody is depending on you. Do you really want to give all of that up? Think about that before you give all of this up and if you are feeling down about being alone, think about this: many of your friends are probably jealous of you and wish they could be single again.

Too many people drift into mediocre relationships that don't really satisfy them and stay there for years (even decades) just because they are afraid of being alone. Before you can have a successful relationship you need to lose that fear. Spend some time alone and learn to enjoy it. Realise that you don't need anyone else to make you happy – you can make yourself happy, at any time. You just need to know yourself and what makes you happy – for me, although I've travelled the world I've realised it only takes a few simple things: a good book, a nice café, a walk by the sea and spending time with my friends. The pleasure of sex is amazing but it lasts for a certain number of minutes and then you have to spend the rest of the day with that person.

Understanding your own value

It's a cliché that we're all unique, but obviously it's true. If someone replaced you with someone else that looked identical, people that know you would notice very quickly. We all have our own characteristics and talents. What's important to understand is that what may be attractive to some people is a complete turn-off to others. That doesn't mean that it's bad or something you need to change. If some brainless party girl at a bar doesn't like you, that doesn't mean you're worthless or of "lower value" than the guy that she likes that is just as dumb as her. You may be very attractive and interesting to someone else, who you probably have more in common with anyway. Take into account constructive criticism, but don't give too much importance to the opinions of people that don't like you and don't care about you. Instead, find people that like you and appreciate you for who you are. What you are seeking is seeking you.

Mistakes to Avoid

Not Trying / Playing it safe

The biggest mistake you a can make as a man is to not try and instead just wait for girls to approach you. It is the only real way to guarantee failure. Nothing else you do could ever be worse than that. When I look back, all of my regrets are the things I didn't say, the girls I didn't talk to or the opportunities I missed because I was too shy to make a move. I don't regret any of the moves I did make, even when I got turned down in the worse possible way, because these are all just experiences that I learnt from. At the very least I learnt that a particular girl was not worth pursuing and you get a bit of practice which will make you better next time – afterwards you can analyse what you did wrong and how you could improve your approach. But you can't learn anything from doing nothing.

Don't take the safe path – be daring and don't worry about what people might think or what people might say if they see you fail. The times when I did act (even when I thought the girl wouldn't like me) I was often very surprised how positive the reaction was. Sometimes girls weren't interested and in this case I could feel the satisfaction of "at least I tried." Often they were even very kind about it – one girl working in a café once told me that she was married, but that I had made her day by talking to her and asking her out. If you play it safe to avoid rejection you will get very little success in dating and meeting women and that is 100% guaranteed. Plus, you will never learn anything.

I know you might want to protect yourself and your feelings but what are you really afraid of? Getting hurt and getting rejected actually makes you stronger, because you learn to deal with it and brush it off. You can develop thick skin and learn not to care about someone else's harsh words. Obviously if someone is nasty then they are not worth dealing with anyway and you found out what you needed to know about them, which was the point in talking to them in the first place. So really you should count it as a success rather than a failure. You were looking for information and you got it and if you continue to move forward that way in the world, success is guaranteed.

Oneitis / Obsession

This is another very common mistake. What happens is you meet a girl, you start to like her and she initially gives you positive signals but at some point either you screw up or she decides (for whatever reason) that she isn't interested anymore. Maybe she found out that you don't like cats or you don't have a BMW. Some girls can be incredibly picky. Or maybe she met another guy that she likes more.

Whatever it is, the problem is that by this point you've already started to imagine this girl in your life and built up a series of expectations and fantasies based on the relationship that you were expecting to develop. This happens mostly to young and inexperienced guys. To me, it happened a lot when I was a kid and now it really doesn't happen so much because I've learnt not to build up too much expectation and also to move quickly. However, it can happen to anyone.

If you move fast then you can lessen the likelihood of someone else moving in on the girl whilst you hesitate and you avoid building up too many feelings without knowing where you stand. If you know from the beginning that a girl doesn't like you then you are not going to get attached to her and have this oneitis.

How women love differently to men

It is said that men love women for who they are, whilst women love men for what they can do for them. I believe this is true, because I have seen it proven to me many times in many different relationships. This is why a woman can seem very much in love with you, but quickly fall out of love as soon as she realises that you can't provide her with what she wanted (which could be anything, but for example might be protection, security, stability, status, reputation, children, marriage or a certain lifestyle etc). It can be kind of shocking when the girl that you thought loved you so much suddenly doesn't love you anymore but this happens. Obviously if she suggests becoming friends it's best to say thank you but no thank you and just get on with your life without her.

The Grey Zone

Some girls are experts at keeping you in the grey zone, where you don't know where you stand. They like to do this because they know that if they tell you or show you that they're not interested then you will stop giving them attention, validation and (if you're really inexperienced or naïve) doing all kinds of favours for them. Don't let a girl keep you in the grey zone. Always insist on meeting alone, escalate and see how far you can get before they make you stop. Get them to put up or shut up. Don't compliment them too much, don't give them lots of attention and don't spend time talking to them on

Facebook, on the phone or by text message. Ask them to meet you alone in person and if they are too busy for that then don't talk to them and don't spend time doing them any special favours.

How to Know When To Go For The Kiss

The first time I went on a date with a girl, I was feeling nervous the whole time because I wanted to kiss her but I didn't know if I could/should do it. The mistake I was making was trying to take one huge leap rather than lots of small steps. It's not necessary to put yourself through this. Instead just take things step by step and you'll find that it's actually very easy to kiss a girl, because by the time you go for it you will already know if she wants you to.

To give an example of this – years later I was standing with a beautiful Sicilian girl in the corner of a bar. We had been talking ever since her friend had introduced us. We went to the bar together and as we walked back to our corner with our drinks I put my arm on her back to guide us through the crowd. When we stopped I found myself looking at her mouth and she gazed back at mine and I realised I still had my hand around her waist and in fact I was now feeling her bum. I pulled her closer and we kissed.

Here, rather than feeling nervous I already knew she would let me kiss her. That is because of how she was letting me touch her and the way she was looking at me. If I had been just standing next to her without touching at an appropriate distance then I would never have got these signals. When you do things this way it just happens naturally without having to think too much about it. You touch more and more and at a certain point you will know that the girl wants you to kiss her.

Avoiding bad relationships

One more warning: it's better to be alone than in a negative relationship. Every day you should think about whether the relationship you are in is positive or negative for you. If it is negative you should end it. Don't waste your life with someone that brings you down. If you know what you want in life, understand your own value and you are not afraid of being alone (for a while), this shouldn't be too hard.

Major Problems

If you have some kind of serious problem that is stopping you from meeting women, before anything else you need to deal with this. This could be, for example: being overweight, having bad fashion, bath teeth or a bad haircut, social anxiety, never going out or living in a boring suburb with your parents. It's better to focus on fixing these problems before you worry about anything else, as otherwise it will like trying to drive a car around with the handbrake on and you will just get bad and discouraging results.

Where to meet girls

Online Dating

Obviously, this depends what kind of girls you want to meet. These days, half the world is online, but that doesn't mean that dating websites are the place to go. Generally for men these are a total waste of time. There are exceptions: if you are young and very good looking (make-model standard), you could do well here.

Here's why online dating is generally a waste of time for men:

When a man puts up a profile, unless he looks like a model, he can expect to receive zero messages per month. A woman, on the other hand, even if she is just of average looks, can expect to receive hundreds of messages and a beautiful woman will receive thousands of messages. What are the chances that a girl will reply to you? Even if she does notice your message that came in together with thousands of others, you have to be super entertaining otherwise she'll soon lose interest and forget who you are.

Anyone that sets up a profile on a dating website should set up two accounts: one as themselves and another as a female. See how many messages each account gets and you'll understand the situation.

Otherwise it's a bit like going into a bar blindfolded and not realising that it is full of men.

Why is it such a negative situation? Well, my theory is that it is related to the fact that men are generally expected to approach women and not vice-versa. The men that don't have the confidence to do this go online and start spamming girls with cut and paste messages telling them how beautiful they are. Either they choose one guy that they like and then leave the site or they get overwhelmed by the amount of messages and leave. Either way, you have about a 1/1000 chance of a beautiful girl responding to you.

Why do men send out these spam messages? Well, if a man only sends out a few personalised messages they probably won't get a reply. If they send 100, maybe they'll get a couple. So it's hardly worth investing their time to read through thousands of boring female profiles, which are mostly a long list of unrealistic preferences, selfish demands or the interests of women that they have never met and probably will never meet. On the other hand, an obvious spam message is likely to just be ignored. It's best to think of something different and interesting to say, maybe a bit surprising and provocative without being rude.

Again, if you are really exceptionally handsome you may have better results. If you really want to make a go of this, find the best photos you have of yourself and make try to make your profile a little bit interesting and mysterious. Don't write too much about yourself and avoid saying anything negative. Don't get discouraged if you don't get any results though - online dating really sucks. As if things weren't bad enough already, a lot of these dating sites are full of fake female profiles set up by the employees of the sites themselves to lure in hungry males and they make it difficult to actually have a conversation without paying them.

Other Websites

I would suggest that, if you do want to meet women online, it is much better to avoid dating websites completely and instead meet women (and people in general) through websites set up based on common interests. For example, Couchsurfing is very good for meeting girls that like travelling, as well as for meeting new people and making friends in general. The good thing about this website is that you quickly get to actually meet the girls rather than wasting time talking with them online whilst they compare you against 1000 other guys. Then, if you like each other, you have a chance to make something happen.

Moving things forward

Wherever you meet girls, meeting is only the first step. Once you are talking to a girl and she feels comfortable with you (i.e. she knows something about who you are, your background etc) then you can start to show your interest in her. It's best to do this when you are alone together in order to avoid her from feeling embarrassed in front of whoever else is there. Depending on her culture, she may reject you in public just because she feels uncomfortable in front of other people or other people may interfere and cause an awkward situation. So you should try to find a way to get the girl to be alone with you. "Alone" can be relative, i.e. a quiet corner of a bar away from her friends etc.

Isolation

The point is you want to get away from being in a group situation and with her one-on-one. Try to avoid having other people around as much as possible. Don't sabotage yourself by bringing along a friend or encouraging her to invite other people. Also, don't take her to a place where either of you know people. That just increases the chances that someone will butt into your conversation and suddenly you'll find yourself sitting far away from her with an annoying fatty that wants to know everything about you whilst she talks to your friend. Find a way to get her alone with you, or at least talking to you one-on-one. At that point you can move on to the next stage.

Becoming an orbiter

Sometimes a girl would really like to keep you around as her "soldier", "orbiter" or "male girlfriend". These are guys that a girl isn't interested in, but she likes to keep around because it feels good to have guys liking her Facebook posts, telling her she's beautiful, listening to her talk about her problems and offering to help her out. These girls really want to keep you in the "grey area" and make you think you have a chance with them, so they tend to avoid explicitly rejecting guys but at the same time they make sure that guys never get the chance to be alone with them. For this reason, they love to hang out in groups or meet in public places.

You may notice that beautiful girls tend to have a lot of these guys around. If you look at a girl's Facebook posts, see how many guys compliment her every time she posts a picture of herself. The prettier the girl (and the more vain she is), the more the orbiters. Don't be an orbiter. There is no better way of wasting your time getting nowhere and making yourself feel worthless. Escalate quickly, find out what you need to know and if a girl is not interested then stop seeing her. If a girl starts asking you to do favours for her, this is a sign that she wants you to be her "soldier". Ask her to come around and see you at your place and if she doesn't come, forget it.

Cockblocking strategies

If I girl doesn't like you, she will either cockblock you herself or get other people to cockblock you. If she likes you, she won't. It's that simple. However, girls often want to keep their team of orbiters and soldiers around as these guys make her feel good and can be very useful to her whenever her toilet backs up or she needs someone to lift some heavy boxes, a free place to stay or a nice free meal.

Therefore, some girls like to cockblock you whilst not being too obvious about it. They don't want to do anything with you but they don't want you to give up and forget about them. So here are some of their strategies:

Always turning up with friends (her cockblocking team)
Meeting you alone but then wanting to go to places where her friends are

Always sitting far away from you or with an obstacle in between (sitting on another couch, across a wide table or putting objects in between you)
Meeting only in public places
Writing to you occasionally but avoiding any "personal" subjects

Obviously the opposite is also true: a girl that always turns up to meet you alone, sits close to you and is willing to come back your place or somewhere equally private is probably interested in you.

Seeing what you want to see

If you really like a girl, there is a danger that you read too much into every small sign of interest whilst ignoring the facts – that this girl is always too "busy" to meet or sits far away from you and avoids being alone with you in any private place. Try to be objective and if necessary, ask your friends for an opinion. This also comes from taking too much time to make a move. If you do it quickly, then you will not get attached before you know how the girl feels about you.

Verbally stating your interest in a girl (love letters)

This is a very bad idea, especially if you do it by text, email or some type of messenger. Back when I was young and naïve, I used to think that this was a great way to express my interest in a girl because it avoided risking rejection. However, I have scientifically proved (so you don't have to) that doing this almost always results in the girl either just ignoring your message or never talking to you again. Not helpful. In fact, even getting a clear "no" would be much better.

The reason for this is that, when you state your interest by some form of message, you are putting the girl in a situation where the easiest thing to do is just to ignore you. They don't want to have an awkward conversation, which they might expect if they turned you down. Also, even if they like you to some degree, they might not want to be forced to state it explicitly. Unless they really are very attracted to you, they will probably just not reply. That is what you should expect and, by doing this, you will kill you chances with women that might have responded if you had just met them and escalated when you had the chance.

Text Messages

Generally speaking, the less the better. Any messages should be as brief as possible and focus on arranging a meeting (alone and in person). Don't get distracted. If she asks about other things, just don't reply and then later say you were busy and get back to arranging the meeting. If you have long conversations by text or Facebook it is highly likely that the girl will lose interest in you or you will say the wrong thing at some point, given that you can't see how she is responding. It also gives the impression that you have nothing else going on in your life.

Flaking

Flaking is when a girl agrees to meet you but later changes her mind and either doesn't show up or texts you some kind of excuse. If this happens, it's obviously a sign of low interest and you should re-evaluate whether it's worth making any effort to meet this girl in the future. As a general rule, if she cancels and doesn't suggest meeting another time then she's probably not interested in meeting you at all.

If you are getting a lot of no-shows, you can do what the airlines do and start overbooking. By this, I mean arrange a lot of meetings in one day so that if one girl doesn't turn up another will. However, make sure you leave the meetings far enough apart so that you don't end up sabotaging the first date just when it was stating to go well to go and meet someone else. If you are meeting a girl for the first time, a 1 hour coffee could turn into spending the whole afternoon together.

I wouldn't recommend more than 3 meetings in a day, ideally at least 5 hours apart. Have some excuse ready about what you have to do later (don't tell them you're going to meet another girl). The worse thing you could possibly do is let the two of them meet – if you do that then you won't get anywhere with either of them.

Logistics

Before going out with a girl, give some thought to how you are going to isolate her and get her back to your place. Obviously this is not possible if you are staying in a hostel or with family, but at least you want to take her somewhere where you will have some privacy. Do some reconnaissance beforehand – you don't want to take a girl to a crowded restaurant where she will be sitting on the other side of a wide table. You want to find a cosy, quiet corner somewhere where you can make your moves.

If a girl really likes you, she will likely be willing to come back to your place with some flimsy excuse such as to watch a movie or show her some photos of a trip you made etc. Don't ask ever ask a girl if she wants to come back with you to have sex – it's better to be subtle because girls don't want to commit to something like that. They'd rather just come back with you and "see what happens". Even if you both know it's going to happen, don't talk about it. Depending on how they behave when they are back home with you, you can forget about the pretext pretty quickly.

If a girl does come back with you, you don't want other people around such as flatmates, friends, family etc. You also don't want pictures or personal items belonging to other girls that they might notice and ask you about. So you need a certain amount of preparation. Ideally the place should be impressive – modern, clean and pleasant to spend time in. Otherwise she'll want to leave quickly just because she doesn't like being there. Put a TV music channel on so that you're not sitting there in silence, offer her a drink, and then invite her into your bedroom to look at some photos on your laptop (make sure these things are strategically placed).

How Girls Behave When They Like You

If a girl likes you she will put herself in a situation where you could make a move on her and then she will wait for you to do it (and be disappointed and perhaps even lose interest if you don't). Don't expect a girl to make the move. This is so rare that it is not even worth considering. The most a girl will do is make things easy for you and send out subtle signals that she wants you to make a move. For example, by sitting close to you or going somewhere alone with you, always being keen to meet up, smiling, laughing at all your jokes, asking lots of questions etc.

Sometimes a girl might like you but she has a lot of "conditions" before she is willing to start a relationship and therefore she will spend time bombarding you with interview-style questions. It's better not to let this go on for too long, because the more you tell her the more reasons she has to find fault with you. Try to distract her with physical escalation and don't take her questions too seriously.

Signs a Girl Doesn't Like You

If a girl doesn't like you she will seek to avoid situations where you might be able to make a move, especially if she knows you like her. She won't be available often (the word "busy" is likely to come up), she'll only want to meet for short periods of time in public places, she won't come back to your place on any pretext and she'll try to bring in cockblockers such as her friends or by talking to other people around you.

If a girl pays too much attention to her phone, keeps taking phone calls from other people or has an overconfident or arrogant manner that is also a very bad sign. A girl should be making an effort to make you like her – if she is not making an effort then this means she doesn't really care. A good test of this is to see what happens in moments of silence – does she try to fill it by asking you questions or does she just expect you to find some way to keep her entertained?

Arrogance is a very clear sign that a girl has low interest. If she insists on going to a certain place, doing what she wants to do regardless of your opinion, makes up ridiculous stories, is judgemental or seems to be mocking you then don't waste time with her.

Don't ever miss your chance

If you have the chance to try to make something happen with a girl, do it. Don't let the opportunity pass you by because later you will regret it and you may never get the chance again. If a girl gives you a chance today, don't assume she will still like you next week. Girls move on very quickly and there are always guys hitting on them. If you don't make a move, some other guy will.

How to meet girls in public

When you are out and about, there are lots of opportunities to talk to girls. However, it can be hard to approach and talk to girls that you don't know as you might fear their reaction. This is actually an internal problem. You are capable of going up to someone and speaking to them, you are not incapable. What stops you is your fear, not any physical impediment. If you go up to a girl and speak to her, even if she completely blows you off in the worst possible way, you will actually feel good about it later because you will have overcome your fear. This will make you feel stronger, more powerful and more confident. If you don't talk to her, later you will wonder what could have been and regret not being brave enough to approach her. So don't be afraid, start with baby steps but take a step in the right direction and start talking to girls you see in public when you get the chance. You don't have to say anything special – just be friendly, ask her a few questions and if it goes well then ask for her number. You'd be surprised how positively women respond and also, but equally importantly, how good you feel afterwards even if they respond negatively.

Creating opportunities

Obviously sitting at home all day you are not going to meet many girls. When you go out they won't approach you either, unless you work as a bartender or a musician. Generally women do not approach men. It happens very rarely that they do, but if you rely on this then you are severely limiting yourself. It is far better to create opportunities to interact with women yourself rather than just waiting for something to happen (you'll be waiting your whole life).

Generally the more daring you are, the less competition. Most men won't approach a girl in the street, whereas a waitress is likely to get hit on a lot more and therefore might be less receptive. It doesn't really matter what you say – if you can start a conversation based on whatever situation you are in, you can see if the girl is friendly and if she is then maybe ask her some questions about herself and invite her out for a coffee / drink or to do something together. At this point she knows that you like her - there's no need to explicitly say it. She might tell you she has a boyfriend or make some kind of excuse. In that case just say "that's OK, it was nice meeting you, thanks for your help" and continue on your way. Whatever the outcome, you should feel happy because you did something that most men can't do and this will give you far more opportunities than the average guy.

Tilting the balance in your favour

It's no secret that certain countries and certain cities are easier than others. Generally your own country is the most difficult, because there you are just another normal guy whereas abroad you are interesting just because you are a foreigner. A guy from Northern Europe will probably do better in Italy, Spain and other southern countries whilst an Italian will do better in northern countries. White Europeans and Americans do well in Asia and South America.

When it comes to going up to and approaching women on the street, this is easy in some countries and extremely difficult in others. In Morocco or the Philippines, women are pretty friendly and open to being approached. It is rare that they will react in an unfriendly way. In Spain and Italy if you can get a girl's attention they will generally be friendly, although you might have to compete with their iPhone. In Turkey they probably not understand you unless you speak Turkish and then once she does understand she will give you an angry and hostile stare and call all of the men within a radius of 100m to come and cockblock you. Maybe I'm exaggerating a bit there, but you get the idea. The differences between countries are huge.

In more difficult countries you need more of a pretext to make an approach and you need to come in more under the radar, whereas in other places you can be far more direct. People in London, for example, are pretty suspicious of anyone that approaches them that doesn't already know them. You could be sitting next to the perfect girl for half an hour and not say a word to her, even if you both like each other. Try to think of a pretext to start an innocent conversation. Ask her a question about how to get somewhere, even if you already know. After that, ask something about her (for example "are you from Spain?") and see if she is interested in continuing the conversation. Yes, other people will look at you but only for a second. Most of them will get off at the next stop anyway and the people that get on after won't know that you guys just met. Maybe it could lead somewhere and maybe not, but do you want to be kicking yourself all day about what could have been?

In all likelihood a girl in a place like London will just answer your question and then get back to her book or her phone. That doesn't make it easy. But you can judge from her initial reaction if she's worth talking to – does she smile, is she helpful and polite or rude and arrogant. It she's friendly, you can try to keep the conversation going by, for example, telling her something about yourself. Again, if she's not interested then just say "thanks" and forget about her but give her a chance - maybe she is interested but initially shy and surprised to find someone talking to her.

The third part of this, once you have managed to ask a random question and asked her a few questions about herself is (if she is friendly) to give her your card or telephone number and suggest that you could meet up somewhere for a drink or a coffee some time. You have to be quick, because within 5-10 minutes she'll be getting off the train, so you can't wait until the last moment. You could be having a great conversation and then she suddenly says "oh, nice talking to you, I have to get off here" and then she's gone forever. So make sure you give her your number before that happens, even at the risk of seeming a bit forward (if she likes you, she won't mind). For situations like this it helps to always some business cards with your number on them – you can get some very impressive ones printed for less than 5 dollars.

In other countries all you have to do is start a conversation and then you'll be asked lots of questions about where you're from, what you're doing there etc. That makes it much easier because all you have to do is mention something you're doing later and invite her along. For example you can say you were just going to grab a coffee, would she like to come?

Good places for meeting women

Hostels are a great place for meeting women because it's easy to start to a conversation, given that you are both travelling and you have something in common that you can talk about straight away. It's pretty normal to say hi and then start a conversation with anyone you meet in your dorm room or around you at the breakfast table. On the other hand you can expect lots of competition and, a bit like at high school, people tend to quickly band together into groups. The difficult thing in this case is making the conversation go further but probably the best way is to suggest visiting some sites together. That way you'll have more time to get to know the girl. As always, you need to be alone with the girl before anything can happen, even if that means just sitting in a corner away from the rest of the group.

Other good places are airports, bookstores, cafes and large ferries or cruise ships. You need to develop the ability to strike up a conversation based on whatever situation you are in. You can practice this with other people - not just women. Then, when a beautiful girl is standing next to you, you can ask her "Are you Korean?" or whatever comes to mind without being too nervous and out of your comfort zone.

Striking up random conversations is really a habit that you can develop, as is the habit of being very touchy-feely, which is really very important to let a girl know you're interested and avoid her seeing you as a guy that just wants to be friends. I found that I got so into the habit of touching that I started doing it even with women I didn't really like that much. It just becomes automatic and you become very sensitive to the responses you are getting as well. There were times in the past when I could just "feel" that a girl liked me. I didn't know how I knew, but I knew. Now, if I look back I can see it was mainly her body language – a smile, the fact that she sat close to me or paid more attention to me than other people, the way she looked at me or laughed at everything I said etc.

Bars and Discos

Men go to these places to get laid. It can work, but it can also be a big disappointment and a waste of time and money. This really depends a lot on your personality. Do you enjoy spending your time (and money) in these places? Do you have fun there and are you able to easily start up a conversation with girls despite their initial resistance? If not, maybe you need a drink. Still can't do it? In that case maybe this is not the place for you. There is no point doing more of what doesn't work. If you're not having any success try changing different factors - your dress, the type of bars and discos you go to, how you approach, who you go out with... perhaps even the cities and countries you go out in. But if it isn't working, don't waste your money. Beers and nightclub covers are expensive and if you're not having a good time then focus on a different strategy. Still go out to enjoy yourself, go to places where you like the music and the atmosphere is fun, but don't make it all about meeting women. They aren't the only places to meet women or even necessarily the best places.

Work, college and university

Work is probably a bad place to meet women in general, but on the other hand for some people it could be a goldmine. Working as a DJ, bartender or some other environment where you are surrounded by young women in the mood for a hook up is a sure winner. Other less obvious ones could be working as an English teacher in a foreign country or working in a gym. Even working in a shop that caters to women can get you some attention.

Of course, you are should be careful when dealing with customers because you represent the company and your behaviour could reflect badly on them. Therefore, you have to be a bit more cautious than normal and try to keep all interactions away from the establishment. If a girl you like shows interest (by being especially friendly or coming back and talking to you several times, for example) then get her number and arrange to meet some time away from where you work. When dealing with colleagues the need for caution is even greater – some companies have policies which forbid dating co-workers. Personally, I think it's none of a company's business to tell me who I can date, but there you go. It's best in any case to be very careful about expressing any interest in a colleague because the slightest misstep could land you in the HR office. If you do end up there, you can take if from me that asking "who lit the fuse on your tampon?" tends to make things worse.

What to do if you get a negative reaction

If a girl is rude or unpleasant, the best thing you can do is just walk away. It's not worth getting into an argument or a fight about it. Most people, even when they are not interested, are considerate enough to be respectful. As for those that are not – you are not missing anything worth having. On the other hand don't let someone walk all over you – if they are rude you have no obligation to continue to be friendly towards them or to stay there listening to them spouting off.

Too good to be true

The opposite can also be the case – a beautiful woman approaches you, smiles and gives you all of the signals that she is interested in you. She stands close, brushes up against you, starts asking questions and basically does everything that this book recommends for guys to do. It may be your lucky day, but maybe not. This is not normal behaviour for a woman, unless you are rich and famous or incredibly handsome. Use common sense here: if you are 50 years old or not very good looking and a hot 20 year old girl approaches you in this way, be a bit suspicious. Chances are she wants something – either money or she could be leading you into some kind of a trap. Just because a woman is beautiful it doesn't mean she is automatically trustworthy or harmless. Criminals often use beautiful women as bait to lure gullible men into their rip-off joints.

Taking it slow

You might sometimes meet a girl and be totally blown away by her beauty. As men, we have that weakness. Nothing else matters – you want this girl. But that doesn't mean you should jump straight into a relationship. If she likes you and get along, that's wonderful but at this point you should make sure that you get to know her before making any kind of long-term commitment such as letting her move into your place (which is a point of no return because it can't easily be undone). You don't know yet if she's crazy, super jealous, a drug addict or a compulsive liar. The time to find out what problems she has is *before* she moves in, not after. And be aware that people can hide this stuff very well. It can take months for some problems to show up.

Some guys even recommend not letting girls know where you live. I think it's not a problem if your accommodation is somewhat temporary or if you know the girls you are bringing back well enough to know they are not crazy. But if you are having lots of short-term relationships with girls you hardly know and these girls know where you live then you could be putting yourself at risk. They could turn up at any time of the day or night, damage your car or make a scene in front of your neighbours. I've heard of women breaking down doors and then accusing the guy of assault.

Red Flags

Here are some major red flags to look out for when you start a new relationship with a woman:
- Doesn't have a job or a source of income (this will get very expensive for you, very quickly)
- Says negative things about her ex-boyfriends/husband (probably one day she'll be telling the same stories about you and painting herself as the victim. Don't automatically believe her side of the story. Remember that the guy she's talking about hasn't had the opportunity to state his case and it's in her interests to make him look bad)
- Comes from a very conservative culture or is serious about religion (this is going to mean no sex or severe limits on what

you can do, as well as problems down the road if you want to have children or get married)

- Has lots of serious problems (because these problems will become your problems and you will have to deal with them)
- Tells lots of lies or unlikely stories
- Says "I love you" far too quickly (before she really knows you)
- Extreme jealousy or rage (it will get worse as time goes on)
- Wants you to buy her expensive things or pay her bills
- Doesn't listen
- Always thinks that she is right
- Doesn't want to pay for anything and expect you to pay all the time on dates

The Contract

At some point when a new relationship begins, the girl will tell you her conditions and present you with a contract. This is a verbal contract, so you might just think that this is idle conversation but in her mind this moment actually marks the beginning of your relationship and to her (although she doesn't say it) it means something like "OK, we can have a relationship, if...". For example, she might say something like "promise that you'll never X" or "promise me that you'll always X". Another type of contract is "I don't want a serious relationship" or "I don't want to just mess around". A girl won't say anything like this to you until she decides that she wants to have a relationship with you, because this defines the terms of the relationship. Try to notice it and take it seriously because if you break these conditions the relationship is likely to end. If you disagree, you might need to renegotiate the terms of the relationship or consider ending it yourself.

Scams

There are quite a few scams going around related to the world of dating. So that you don't fall into the trap, I will describe a few of them.

The Chinese "English conversation" scam: in cities like Beijing and Shanghai, any single guy is likely to be approached by women that seem friendly, ask you where you are from and then suggest that you could go to have tea together because they want to practice their English with you. If you go with them they will lead you to somewhere that looks like a normal café but when you get the bill it will be for hundreds of dollars and at this point you will notice that their are some nasty-looking thugs that won't let you leave until you pay.

Latvian bar scam: this is similar to the Turkish scam, except that in this case the victim is usually a single guy that is approached by a pair of beautiful women either at or outside a bar and it involves taking you to a fake disco/bar where the prices are 10 times what could be considered reasonable and then ordering lots of drinks. These women also hang out inside certain bars and discos and get men to come with them by saying "let's go to another place I know".

The black widow scam: frequent in hotel bars around the world, this involves a woman coming back to your hotel room and slipping something into your drink whilst you are out of the room. You fall into a deep sleep and she has all the time she wants to take anything of value such as money, credit cards, laptop, phones and even your passport. If you do meet a girl, especially if she is the one approaching you, don't let things move forward too quickly – take your time getting to know them. If it seems too good to be true, be very careful. If they are in a really big hurry to get back to your room, take some precautions such as, for example, going to another hotel and leaving your money etc in the hotel safe at reception. Be suspicious if someone insists on serving you a drink and see what happens if you swap the glasses before drinking up.

Romance Scams

A Romance Scam is when someone pretends to love you or want a relationship with you in order to extract something of value from you, which in most cases is money or gifts but may also be your assistance in getting a visa, residence or nationality in your country of origin. Unfortunately some men completely lose their senses when a beautiful woman tells them what they want to hear and they believe that they really are in a relationship with this person. This section goes into some of the typical ways that these scammers behave so that if you see this behaviour you can recognise it more easily.

I love you > Sob story> Send money

This is the basic formula. A girl wants you to believe she has feelings for you so that she can get you into a "relationship" with her. Then, once she knows she has you hooked, she will start making up sob stories to get you to feel sorry for her and to give her money.

1. I love you / I need you / I can't live without you etc.
2. I have a problem / I'm ill / I had an accident / I got robbed / I got raped / My family chucked me out of the house
3. I need money for rent / medicine / taxi / doctor etc.

If you notice this pattern, then be very cautious and ask the opinion of your friends and relatives who can perhaps see the situation more clearly than you as they are not emotionally involved. If someone that you hardly know tells you they love you, be suspicious. If they follow that up with a sob story, you can guess what is coming next... they will start asking you for money.

Romance Scams in the Philippines

The Philippines is known for a variation of the "I love you" scam which is mostly done online, through online dating sites. Basically young women (and in some cases older women or men pretending to be young women) target men on dating sites and (once they've established an online "relationship") start hitting them up for money. Generally they target older men because they know they are richer and more likely to be "generous". It's pretty easy for them to pull it off because all they have to do is go to an internet café, put up some photos, talk to a few guys and after a while start telling them their sob stories. Pretty soon, they are collecting hundreds of dollars at the Western Union across the street. Their friends will advise them on how to come up with the best sob stories and these can be fairly elaborate. For example: they don't have money for school books or to pay for their examples, their mother is sick, their buffalo died etc.

This is a huge industry in the Philippines and technically it's not even really illegal, because as far as the local police are concerned you are just a fool that sent money to a woman as a gift. In any case, you would have to be in the country and know the (real) name and address of the person that scammed you in order to get anything done about it and even then the police won't care. I wouldn't advise meeting up with your scammer. You may think that you're dealing with an innocent young woman but may actually be dealing with some hardened criminals in some cases. Incidentally try not to get into arguments in the Philippines - generally it doesn't turn out too well for foreigners, who often (sometimes with the help of the police) end up getting shaken down for a lot of money.

I would highly advise reading about other people's experiences online if you have any suspicions about any online relationship you have in which someone that you don't know very well or have never met in person is asking for money. I'm not saying don't get involved with girls from the Philippines – they can be wonderful, but if you get any requests for money be very suspicious. Don't get taken for a fool.

Romance Scams in Thailand

In Thailand, there is a similar type of scam but it tends to be related to "working girls" that get into relationships with foreigners in order to extract money from them. Unlike prostitutes elsewhere, many prostitutes in Thailand know that they can get more out of a man if they are patient and act like a girlfriend rather than demanding money upfront. If you ever sit in an internet cafe in somewhere like Sukhumvit Road in Bangkok you can see women writing the same message to 6 different guys in various countries: "darling, how are you? I miss you so much. My mum she sick, please send me money…"

Before going to Thailand or whilst you are there, I highly recommend reading some books on the subject. One very good one is "Hello My Big Honey" which describes the situation very well and includes a collection of love letters between foreign men and their Thai girlfriends. My favourite was one from a German man that complained that every time he said "I love you" she would reply "buy me television" or "give me money" and he was starting to suspect that she didn't love him as much as he loved her. Unfortunately it's not normally that obvious. Of course that is not to say that all women in Thailand or anywhere else are bad. Just exercise some common sense – if you met a woman in a bar (i.e. a brothel) don't believe automatically believe everything she says.

I'm pregnant

Here, a girl pretends to be pregnant and, if she's managed to hook you as one of her "boyfriends" then she'll ask you to pay for the abortion or the hospital. Some girls can go so far as to bribe fake or real doctors to provide the paperwork showing that they are pregnant. In some cases, the girl may actually be pregnant, whether deliberately or otherwise, and the father could be anyone. This gives her the opportunity to extort you, or perhaps even convince you to do the "right thing" by marrying her - giving her a visa for your country and access to half of everything you own. Not a good idea! Don't marry anyone unless you want to and you are sure that you really know and trust this person. Don't even consider marrying someone of dubious character – this is a guaranteed way of ruining your future and your life. You can avoid all of this by not getting involved with these kinds of people in the first place.

Marriage Fraud (for immigration purposes)

It is almost impossible for people from some countries to get a visa for Europe or America. Some people will probably never leave their country in their lifetimes, and everyone knows life is a lot better abroad. So for them, their country is like a jail and you could be their ticket out! If you're wondering why so many beautiful young girls are so keen marry you, here's why: free language classes, a free flight, a free place to live, spending money and, after a few years, a foreign passport.

Marriage in General

Another great way of ruining your life is getting married to the wrong person. It can take you 30 years to save up and acquire a house, a nice car and a comfortable way of life. Marrying the wrong person can see you lose all of that very quickly. And marrying the "right" person can have the same effect if, for whatever reason, the marriage doesn't last.

Before making the decision to marry someone, make sure that you know them very well and ideally, they should be at approximately the same economic level as yourself. The reasoning for this is that if they earn or have less money than you then they stand to gain from divorcing you. From the moment you marry, there will suddenly be a huge financial incentive for them you leave you. Imagine if right now, you were offered $300,000 if you left your girlfriend for someone else. Would that make you more or less likely to stay loyal? This is the incentive you are offering when you get married – a big fat cash incentive to leave you, plus (in some places) monthly payments called alimony which is something like a monthly salary for having been with you in the past. If you have children, you will pay child support on top of all of this, which is a percentage of your salary. For example, if you earn 100k per year, she will get an extra 30k per year to spend on handbags and shoes. Think about all of that before you sign the contract, which is what marriage is.

Anyone that does get married should definitely get a prenuptial agreement to avoid getting raped in divorce court 2 or 5 or 10 years later, which has at least a 50% chance of occurring. This agreement needs to be drawn up by a lawyer and a lawyer representing her should also be present, otherwise it will simply be declared invalid when the time comes.

Getting Used as a Source of Free Food and Drink

If you invite a girl out and she arrives with someone else (her friend / sister / cousin etc) then she is likely just interested in spending as much of your money as possible and her friend is there to help her do so twice as fast. Tell her you just brought enough money with you for a coffee and don't let her order anything expensive. If necessary, explain to the waiter that you are not going to pay for any food. Alternatively, you could just walk out. I was once with a girl like this and when she went off to buy cigarettes I ate her lunch and finished her drink and when she came back she found me paying the bill. When she came back I said "I thought that you had left".

In some countries dating etiquette requires the man to pay. Generally in Europe this is not the case, but it is so in the USA, Latin America and many parts of Asia. However, this can lead to being taken advantage of if you're not careful, so make sure that you don't spend more than you want to spend and that if you're paying then you decide exactly where you want to go. Don't let someone else lead you around to expensive places where they want to eat and drink at your expense.

Investigation

It would be wrong to look at your girlfriend's Facebook account to see who she's talking to so I wouldn't advise doing that even if you are suspicious, simply because it would be so wrong. Even if she leaves her Facebook open on her computer (as girls often do) don't look at it. Even worse would be installing some kind of keylogger on her computer to see what she's up to, so make sure that you don't ever do that.

Don't rush in

You may think that you've got it bad now. You are whatever age and still a virgin or you have been single for however many months or years. But there are guys that would love to be in your shoes right now – young, free, with no commitments or financial obligations (child support, alimony, payouts to the ex-wife etc). So enjoy being single and use the time to improve yourself, learn new things, travel and take advantage of the opportunities that present themselves. Don't rush into a relationship just to avoid being alone.

Living together

Before you start to live with a woman understand one thing: the moment you start living together your freedom is over. Don't take this decision lightly. Once you have a woman living in your home she will know what you are doing, where you are and who you are with practically 24 hours a day. By default it makes your relationship exclusive and you can forget about talking to other girls. Also, it is much easier to take this step forward than to reverse it. Once she's in, making her leave (or leaving yourself) pretty much spells the end of the relationship. You won't be able to just go back to how things were before.

Women that don't work

Be careful with any woman that is not gainfully employed. Try to get an idea of a woman's plans for the future and particularly how she plans to make a living. If she has no plan, a very vague plan or an unrealistic plan then it is highly likely that she expects you to "take care" of her, which means paying for everything she wants forever. This will instantly cut your salary in half and in some cases (if she spends a lot) you could be left with less than half. Also, don't underestimate to what extent a person that doesn't have to work for money is capable of wasting. This can be a huge drain on your budget, so be very cautious before you accept to take on this kind of burden.

Women that work too much

The opposite can also be a problem. If you love to travel and have a job that allows you to do that, getting involved with a woman that works long hours every day and that has to stay most of the year in a city that you don't want to be in is a problem. Either you will have to stay there and get bored (and wait for her at home whilst she goes to work), just to have a few hours per day with her when she'll be tired anyway, or you will spend a lot of time apart which creates its own problems.

Gold Diggers

Even worse than a woman that is lazy and that doesn't want to work are gold diggers. These are women that just want your money, or to live a luxurious and extravagant lifestyle at your expense. It should be pretty obvious if this is what you are dealing with and they generally only target wealthy men, but you do get some that have gold-digging tendencies of different degrees. Just because you are not rich, it doesn't mean you might be an attractive target to a less ambitious gold-digger. The way to smoke them out is to tell them you believe in feminism and therefore women should work and pay for their own expenses. This makes them very angry. Also, make sure they know that you would never be so stupid as to get married without a pre-nuptial agreement.

One of the worse mistakes a man can make in his life is to marry a gold digger. In my opinion a woman that brings zero dollars into a marriage doesn't deserve to walk out with anything and the current marriage and divorce laws are effectively legalising theft. Don't ever sign such a bad default contract, no matter how "offended" a woman pretends to be. If you have more money than the woman you are marrying then a 50/50 splitting of assets on divorce is totally unfair to you. Don't agree to that and make sure a fair agreement is in place before you sign the marriage contract (which should really be called a "sharing of financial resources agreement"). Of course, if you suspect a woman is a gold digger then it's best not to get married and not let her move in with you in the first place. Don't get her pregnant, either.

Cultural Differences and Traditional Gender Roles

Some women don't want to work and expect men to pay for everything. This can be a generalised attitude in some countries, where men are expected to be the breadwinners and women are expected to stay at home and cook and clean. It's a good idea to talk about this subject to your girlfriend about this before taking the step of living together so that you understand her attitude towards money and what she expects from you (and men in general). On the other hand, if you are earning a good salary and don't mind paying for everything as long as she makes you nice food and keeps the house clean, that's up to you – you might even prefer being with a girl from a more conservative society.

Bad Dating Advice

There is a huge industry built up around the idea of giving men dating advice. In my opinion, a lot of it is terrible. Firstly, don't take advice from women. Women will tell you things like "just be yourself", "be nice" or "be romantic". The problem with this advice is that there is a big difference between what women say and what they actually respond to. If you are nice, you'll get taken advantage of and if you are romantic women will laugh at you behind your back. What does "be yourself" mean anyway? Who else could you be?

On the other hand, a lot of the mainstream dating advice has useless ideas like "be confident", "act like you own the place" or "be cocky and funny". Well, you can't just decide to turn confidence on or off as if it were a switch. Nobody went out and decided not to be confident. Confidence is important, yes, but it is something that you build up over time once you have experience. You shouldn't expect to have it right at the beginning and there is no need to pretend otherwise. Just accept where you are right now and understand that you will get better and it will get easier. Consider the failures as a learning experience.

As for "acting like you own the place" when you walk into a bar or club, I think that is also bad advice because it makes it sound like you need to put on some kind of act and pretend to be important. It will only make you feel nervous because instead of relaxing, you are pretending to be something you're not. Of course, if you can afford it why not buy the whole club or disco and you really will own the place.

There is also the common "be cocky and funny". Well, this is another piece of advice that makes it seem like you have to put on some kind of an act and adopt a false personality. This is really not necessary. By all means tell jokes, but only if you enjoy telling them. Serious people can be interesting too. You should realise that your true self is unique and interesting to the right girl and you don't have to be just another guy trying to be cool, pretending he's not shy or nervous, pretending to be confident and pretending to be "the alpha male" or whatever they call it this week.

Instead of all of this nonsense it is better to have a clear idea of who you are, what you want, what your objectives are and how you plan to achieve them. Have respect for yourself and let go of the idea that your value is determined by some girl who could have any number of weird and vain preferences. Don't let other people take you off track or convince you that you need to fit into some kind of standard template in order to be successful. Trying to copy everyone else will only make you less interesting and less attractive. One thing that I find helps me is to think "what would I do if I was more confident?" Then I do that thing. It's a bit like method acting – you imagine what it would feel like / be like and then you play that role.

Another useful exercise, in my opinion, is to look at yourself and think about what you might be doing wrong. If you are feeling ill you don't search on Google for "illness" and expect to find a solution. You need to be far more specific. The same thing with dating – you need to identify the specific areas where you are failing and address those issues. For some people it might be that they just aren't going out and meeting women. For others it could be their dress sense, personal hygiene, being overweight or there could be some aspect of their personality that makes them appear unattractive. You need to identify what this is and you won't find it in a book.

So how can you get this kind of personalised advice? Well, there are dating coaches but these are expensive, especially if you want to talk to them one on one rather than as part of a big group. A better way would be to ask friends that are more successful than you what you think you should change to be more successful with women. Try to get them to be honest and perhaps to observe you and tell you what you did wrong. This will help you to fix your "blind spots" – things that you have maybe been doing your whole life that you didn't know were screwing you up.

A third way is to find out from women, but the problem is you can't ask them directly. The reason is because they'll just bullshit you and give you some useless generic advice. For example, they'll tell you "just be yourself, be generous, friendly and romantic bla bla bla". Of course, behind your back they will tell their friends "oh, I would never date a guy like that, he's too short/fat/ugly/old", "I don't like guys that smoke" or "he has bad breath/body odour" etc. What you need to do is find out what they are telling their friends about you (there are ways and means of find that out) or make them angry so that they will tell you directly. I call this technique "smoking them out of the wood shack". If you are always polite girls will be polite back and they won't want to offend you by telling you the cold hard truth, so sometimes it actually pays to be a bit rude.

You might need to be a bit devious to find out what people are saying about you behind your back but if you can do this is a great way of discovering your blind spots and the good news is that most of these things can be changed or improved once you know what they are.

How to Spend Less on Dates

Some women are only interested in taking advantage of you and spending as much as possible whilst someone else is paying. Unfortunately society often encourages this sort of behaviour. Anyway, the best way to avoid it is to figure out quickly if a girl really likes you and not spend time with her if she doesn't. However, sometimes it's not possible to know for sure so for cases when you do go out with a girl that you're not sure about here is some advice which will save you money.

Choose the location – Don't get a girl tell you where to meet or where to go. Especially don't let her choose an expensive place. If she insists on only meeting you at an expensive restaurant, DTB (dump that bitch). She can eat at an expensive restaurant on her own dime if she wants. It's important to understand that you're not losing anything by dumping her at this stage. If she really liked you she would be happy to go with you somewhere else (except perhaps KFC, McDonalds or the cafeteria at an abortion clinic). The important thing should be the fact that she is meeting you and not which restaurant she's going to.

Don't Order A Meal For Yourself – If you've ignored my previous advice and let the little lady lead you an expensive place where she intends to milk you dry (and not in a good way), you can use this trick to outsmart her and repel her attack on your wallet. What you have to do is tell her you've already eaten and so you're not very hungry. Let her order for herself (but watch her like a hawk and shoot down any attempts to order anything really expensive). Then, when the food arrives, tell her you'd like to try a bit and eat half of it. Few women are shameless enough to try to order again and, even if they do, you can eat half of that as well or just boot them out.

Sob Stories – Be very suspicious if you hear any kind of a sob story from a girl that you're just getting to know. Any request for money, any hint that she needs money or the mention of any kind of problem involving money should be viewed as her trying to put her hand in your wallet. It's another thing if you've been dating for a while and you're the person she comes to for help, but definitely do not give money to any girl that you've only just met recently. It's very likely that her sob stories are confected and used repeatedly with different guys.

Actions, not Words

When you meet someone new (and this does not just apply to dating) you should pay attention to their actions and not their words. If a girl is telling you she can't wait to see you but she always seems to busy to actually meet, you know the deal. To her you are not a priority, no matter what she says. The same is true for a girl that is always in a hurry to leave or who does not make an effort to look good for you and be on her best behaviour. Too much confidence (or arrogance) is a bad thing. It means lack of genuine interest.

Compliance Testing

Apart from physical escalation (which is a type of compliance test in itself), you need to continuously test a girl to see her level of interest by seeing to what extent she is wiling to go along with your plans and suggestions. A girl that likes you is going to be willing to go along with pretty much anything you suggest, whereas a girl that doesn't care about you is going to raise objections, make excuses and generally make things difficult. This includes, especially, threatening that if she doesn't get things her way she won't go out with you or that she will leave you, etc. That in itself is a huge red flag and it's very close to admitting that she is only with you so that she can get that thing that she wants.

The word "Busy"

When you hear this word from a girl, it means she's not interested. It's also a lie, because pretty much everyone is free at some point during the day once they finish work and they could find time to meet you if they really wanted to. If you're so far down their list that they can only meet you once per week then obviously you're not very important to them. Some girls will never tell you outright that they're not interested but they will continuously make excuses until you give up.

Flake Revenge

If a girl flakes on you repeatedly or is always late, apart from taking it as a sign of low interest and no longer making any effort to spend time with her, if she's been really disrespectful it can be fun to get revenge on her. One guy I know set up a date with a girl long after he had left the city and sent her to some faraway location. Of course she arrived unreasonably late as usual and when he started getting calls and texts he just ignored them.

Scammers and Scambaiting

If someone is trying to scam you, then you can turn it around and use their greediness against them. They think that because you like them they can get you to spend money on them or give them money and so they give you a few crumbs of feigned interest and make you think that if you give them what they want then they'll give you what you want. Well, if this is the case then you know what they want (money or gifts) and you can use this as bait to make them waste their time.

I did this once with a girl that was pretending to be interested in me (but obviously wasn't) and kept on bringing up some hard-luck storey about needing to pay for insurance for her apprenticeship. I knew she just wanted money as her replies to my texts were lazy and brief and she was always "busy" (doing what, if she supposedly finished work at 4pm every day?). Anyway, she failed to turn up on a date and didn't even text me to let me know. I hadn't even gone there myself because the location was close to my hotel and I expected her to be late and call me whenever she arrived (a good precaution to take with people that are habitually late).

I thought about it and sent her a message later saying that I had been sitting there with the money in an envelope but she never arrived. Suddenly she wasn't busy anymore and she was ready to meet at the earliest opportunity. At this point I knew for sure she was a scammer that was only interested in getting her hands on my money. I could have sent her anywhere I wanted using the money as bait. Later I describe what I did with her.

Users and Losers

Obviously you need to be able to tell when someone is really interested and when they are not. Any mention of a need for money or some kind of problem that could be resolved with money are a huge red flag, especially when you are just getting to know someone. Someone that really likes you is going to avoiding bringing up these subjects and is not going to want to scare you away at the first meeting by showing how much of a loser they are even if their life really is a mess. In any case, you need to ask yourself whether you want to get involved with someone that can't even take care of their own everyday expenses and is going to be a drain on your finances.

Not sure if they like you?

If you are not sure about the level of interest, then you can do a few tests. Obviously someone that wants to use you is going to tell you that they are interested, so asking them doesn't help. If someone wants to deceive you, they'll tell you whatever they think you wan to hear.

Touch and Proximity - Sit close to them and see how comfortable they are with you touching them. Do they move away or do they touch you back? Do they try to subtly install a barricade with their handbag or coat or go to the bathroom and sit further away when they come back? Someone that really likes you would never do this and they would respond positively or at least not object.

Facial expression – look very carefully at their face. Are they looking at you? Do they look like they're enjoying being with you and interested in what you have to say? Or are they looking around the room or concentrating on their food, their phone or some other distraction. When they look at you, what do you see? It is said that we can lie, but the truth is written on all of our faces. If you see anger, resentment, boredom, contempt or some other unpleasant emotion then don't ignore it. Prod them a bit more and see how they react. It's mainly a question of just paying close enough attention. It's easy to lie but it's hard to fake emotion.

Conversation – have you ever noticed that it's very easy to talk to some girls and with others it's very difficult (there are long pregnant pauses, you run out of things to say, etc)? Generally this is because the girl is not putting any effort into the conversation. Someone that is genuinely interested will be curious about you and ask lots of questions. If someone doesn't ask any questions at all it's most likely because they don't care. They just care what they can get from you. If the girl isn't making a lot of effort to keep the conversation going and asking you questions that's another clear sign of disinterest. If there are lots of long silences, don't keep talking to try to fill them. Instead, take the opportunity to test her by seeing what she does. This will tell you a lot about her interest level.

Text Messages – This is a bit like having a conversation. One-word answers are a sign of disinterest. If you ask someone if they want to meet tomorrow and they just reply with "OK" then I would doubt whether they are going to turn up at all. Two or three "OKs" in a row are a sign that this person is not really paying attention and probably has no intention of being there.

Respect – Someone that likes you is going to be on their best behaviour. They're not going to be rude, making demands or doing anything that a reasonable and considerate person wouldn't do, such as being excessively late, not turning up to a date or cancelling at the last minute.

Confidence – too much confidence, which you could call arrogance, is definitely a bad sign. If someone is not asking themselves the question "do they like me?" then it's because they don't really care. Someone that likes you is going to be at least somewhat concerned about not doing or saying anything that you won't like, so they should be a little self-conscious during the first meetings. If they are arrogant, it shows that they don't really care if they lose you, i.e. you don't matter to them.

Dealing with lateness

It's best to meet in a place where, if you have to wait, you can at least enjoy the wait and do something productive with your time. Therefore it's better to meet in a café with wifi, for example rather than outside a metro station (where you might have to stand there in the cold or the rain for a long time). If someone is late the first time, then the second time you should expect them to be late by the same amount and plan to be there later. For example, if you agree to meet at 10:30 then don't even bother to go there before 11am if they were half an hour late before. If they're on time then they can wait this time, but that's highly unlikely.

If someone is unreasonably late then just leave. Don't tell them that you're leaving though, because since they made you go there and wait then it's only fair that they should also go the whole way there only to find that they wasted their time just as you did. You can stay nearby if it's convenient for you, so that if they arrive and start calling you then can still come back but you should note that extreme lateness is always a sign of disinterest and disrespect, especially if they don't let you know that they will be late.

If someone is disrespectful, then in my opinion they deserve the same treatment. There was one girl I used to meet who was always late so I ended up agreeing to meet her at a certain time and didn't even bother to leave my house until I got her "I'm here, where are you?" text. With another one I would agree to meet early in the morning and still be in bed at that time, knowing that there was no chance she'd actually be there until later. I'd wake up and text her "where are you" to see how late she was and then only then I'd start getting ready.

Dealing with scammers

Just as I feel that disrespectful people deserve to be treated the same way, I think the same about scammers. If someone is wasting my time and trying to deceive me then I have no problem doing the same back to them. In fact, it can be fun. If, for example, a girl starts telling you sob stories about how she needs money for this or that (which is almost certainly a scam), then you can lead her on my making her think you're going to give her money but never giving it to her. I once made a girl go to an Arab restaurant and ask for "Ana Charmouta", who I had left some money with. However Ana is not an Arab name, it is the first person singular so it means "I am" and "Charmouta" means "a whore". After that I sent her to a shopping centre and watched her approach a bunch of guys at Starbuck whilst I sat at Dunkin Donuts.

Once there was a girl that pretended to be interested but had made me suspicious by repeatedly mentioning her money problems and, because I never offered to give her money as she was obviously hoping, she failed to turn up for the next date without even letting me know. I hadn't gone to the meeting place myself anyway because my hotel was nearby and she was always late, but I know she didn't go because she didn't send me any messages. So later that day I messaged her that I had been sitting there with 100 dollars in an envelope but she hadn't turned up.

So now, after seeing the $ signs, she immediately apologized and claimed she had been in the hospital. What did she have, I wondered? "Colds and a headache". I didn't know that it was possible to have more than one cold at once and this poor girl had also had a headache, so it must have been really bad. Of course with several colds and a headache coming all at once she couldn't have been expected to send a text message or call to let me know she wasn't going to come, could she?

The next day I thought about not even bothering to turn up but in the end I did and let her sit there for a while, squirming whilst I questioned her in detail about her supposed hospital visit. She didn't dare to outright ask me for the money but she left after a while and then started writing me angry text messages. I guess she didn't like her own medicine but I think she fully deserved it – after all, she had no problem with wasting my time the day before.

Ending a bad relationship

If you realise at any point that you have made a mistake and got yourself involved in a bad relationship then it's time for some damage control. Firstly, don't make it even worse by taking on more commitments, having more children or getting married. Don't move in together. Make a plan to leave (if necessary consult a lawyer), think about it for a while to make sure that it's really what you want to do and then, when you are ready: do it. Life is too long to spend it doing what someone else wants. Don't let 5 years pass getting increasingly miserable and frustrated. How many periods of 5 years do you have left before you are too old to have the chance to start again? Don't let life pass you by. Success is doing what you want in life and if part of that is meeting lots of different women and have new experiences, don't let anyone stop you.

Dealing with a breakup

Whether it's you or whether it's the other person that ends the relationship, expect it to hurt. It always hurts, even if you are the one leaving. There is always going to be a lot of disappointment, a lot of "what ifs" and wondering if you did the right thing, perhaps some anger and perhaps some guilt. What if I hadn't said this or what if we had stayed together, etc. You have to let it go and stop thinking about it. As soon as you do this you will start to feel better.

The easiest way is to make a clean break. Don't talk to them any more than absolutely necessary, don't keep checking out their Facebook (in fact it can be good to keep away from Facebook for a while) and maybe even block them or reduce channels of communication to just email. Leave one channel open so that you are not left wondering if they are trying to contact you, but don't have them on any kind of instant messenger app otherwise you could end up continuously checking every 5 minutes to see if they sent you a message. This will make it easier to stop thinking about them, which is the key to getting over someone.

It can be helpful to distract yourself with other things, doing activities you enjoy and being with friends and family. But you'll need some time alone to really think about what happened and why it went wrong. You need to process it, accept that it's really over, reflect on what happened and recognise the pain but choose to be happy and to move on with your life. You need to learn the lesson of this failed relationship so that in the future you won't make the same mistake, but not dwell on it for too long. I can be good to take a pen and paper and write about it or write a list of the good and bad qualities of the person that you broke up with, to put it all in perspective and remind you that things were never as perfect as they are in your daydreams.

Try to get past the sadness and the anger before you speak to the person again. Otherwise you might just make the situation worse by saying things that you'll regret later. Don't accept someone that breaks up with you as a friend, because that will just make it harder to get over them. There is no need to be rude, but tell them that you can't be their friend. I like this quote from Rumi about these situations:

"Sorrow prepares you for joy. It violently sweeps everything out of your house, so that new joy can find space to enter. It shakes the yellow leaves from the bough of your heart, so that fresh, green leaves can grow in their place. It pulls up the rotten roots, so that new roots hidden beneath have room to grow. Whatever sorrow shakes from your heart, far better things will take their place."

It's true, ending a relationship involves a lot of pain. But think of it this way - it ended for a reason. It had to end because there was something in that relationship that was seriously wrong, otherwise it surely would have continued. Therefore now you're free again and this time you have more wisdom, experience and knowledge than before. Hopefully the next relationship you have will be better and you will owe the improvement to this painful experience that you're going through now. This is the pain of developing, the pain of growing, and we have all felt it.

Separation Anxiety

Here is a psychological theory that might explain certain situations, especially situations involving breakups. The theory is that anxiety = desire. Therefore in a relationship there always needs to be some level of anxiety otherwise there is no desire. If someone feels too certain that they "have you in their pocket" then they will stop desiring you. That is why doing things like writing love letters and getting emotional with someone who is uncertain about you will only push them away further. If you take away their anxiety then you take away the potential for desire. They really need to feel that are going to lose you forever. The worst thing you could ever do if a girl breaks up with you is to continue to contact her. This will make her feel that can still have you any time she wants, whilst also going out and looking for other men to date.

Even worse is remaining friends with a girl that has broken up with you or rejected you. In this case you are also just showing that she can have you any time she wants, so she doesn't have to worry about how she treats you because she knows that you'll always be there. It's only when she starts to miss you and starts wondering if she'll ever see you again that she might start questioning whether she made the right choice. In any case, being friends with someone that doesn't want you is always a bad deal. At some point, she's going to want to introduce you to her boyfriend or start talking about the other men she's seeing… and why would you want that?

If you get along well with a girl and she's a nice person that you think really would be a good friend if you didn't find her so attractive, then there is an alternative to cutting her off completely. You could just put her in the "time capsule" by not talking to her for 10 years or however long it takes for her to completely lose her looks. Women get fat, get old or just wear themselves out pretty quickly. There are women that I used to be crazy about that I now consider friends and have no problem meeting as friends if I am ever in their town. I don't desire them any more. If I meet their boyfriends, if anything I feel slightly sorry for them. Facebook is quite useful for this. Sometimes I look at photos of women that in the past blew me off or were rude or nasty to me and it gives me some satisfaction to see that I wouldn't want to be with them now anyway. I left them behind and found something better.

Often in breakup situations, when one person sees that the other has finally moved on and no longer wishes to be with them they feel a sudden anxiety that makes them question whether they did the right thing. This anxiety is painful, because it feels like you are being abandoned and this is a very powerful emotion. It's useful to understand what this is and that it is a normal part of breaking up. It doesn't necessarily mean you should get back with that person, just because you want to end the pain. Also, if you let this painful emotion hijack your behaviour you will probably do things that will just make it less likely that the girl will ever want you back, such as making yourself look weak and desperate.

The best way to handle a breakup is to say something like "I'm sorry you feel that way, but if that's what you want I'll respect it". And then never contact them again. If they say something about being friends just say "I could never just be friends with you." The key is that you want to induce separation anxiety in them. You want them to feel that pain and wonder if they are doing the right thing. If you tell them or show them that "you'll always be there" then they are going to feel very comfortable and secure with their decision and find leaving you totally painless. This is why you shouldn't contact them - every time you do, you are taking that pain away and making them feel comfortable with having left you. Not to say that there's any guarantee that this person will come back, but at least you're not helping them along.

Reducing your own separation anxiety

The other part of this theory is that, knowing that your feelings for the person that broke up with you are largely anxiety caused by the separation, obviously you want to minimise this anxiety for two reasons:

- To make the situation easier for you and to help you move on quickly
- To stop yourself from doing things that are going to make you look weak/angry/upset, because these things will only make the situation worse and make you less attractive to your former partner and others.

Knowing that what you are feeling is really just separation anxiety and not "love" makes it easier, because you can treat those anxious feelings and reduce them in the same way as you would treat anxiety with any other cause. For example, eating a big breakfast in the morning has been found to reduce anxiety (something to do with the human fear of not having food to eat, especially when separated from the people that would normally be there for us).

Tips to get over someone quickly

- Don't talk to them and don't spend time with them. Every time you do will only remind you of the fact that you can't be together.
- Block them from any instant messaging apps. Tell them that if they need to speak to you, to send you an email.
- Avoid music in general, and especially any songs that remind you of them.

- Don't delete their photos or destroy any property, but put these things out of your direct line of sight so that you won't be reminded of them every time you get up in the morning or use your computer. Later, once these things have lost their emotional value, you can rationally decide what to do with them.
- Try to avoid saying anything when you are either angry or upset. A useful exercise can be to write a letter or email but not send it. Give it a 24 hour delay and then, the next day, read what you wrote again and see if you still think it's worth sending. Chances are you will probably realise that it's best not to send what you wrote the day before.
- Do some kind of analysis on a piece of paper of the relationship. Write down the positive things, the negative things and, based on that, an evaluation of whether the relationship could have lasted. This will make you look at things in a different way.
- Finally, write a list of all of the things you are grateful for about the relationship that just ended. Think about how lucky you are to have had this experience. And think about what you could have done better and will do better next time.
- If someone that you want a relationship with tells you "let's just be friends", tell them that you're sorry but you can't be their friend and that it's better to stop talking. Give it time and maybe in the future you could actually be friends, but for now it's best not to be.

He who cares less wins

In any relationship (business, personal or just when buying something) the person that cares less wins. This is because they know they could walk away and find the same or a better deal somewhere else. They know that if they look around they could get better price, a better quality item or a better relationship. Therefore they have the upper hand and they are the ones that are going to start dictating conditions that the other person has to comply with. You always need to be the person that cares less. If you find yourself caring too much, stop yourself, because if you continue you will be giving the other person the upper hand and once they know it they will use it against you.

Being in the friendzone is just one example of that. It is a situation where you have a relationship with someone that cares a lot less about you than you do about them. Therefore they have the upper hand and they can make you do anything they want. In some cases guys are buying jewellery, taking women on expensive trips and doing anything they can to impress them in the hopes of getting what they want but it doesn't work. When someone cares less about you than you do about them, the solution is to stop caring or at least to reduce your interest in them to an appropriate level (to the same or less than their level of interest).

A girl that I like that wants to be "just friends" with me is not an important person as far as I'm concerned. They could become a friend eventually if they lose their looks or I just lose interest in ever being with them, but I don't see any value in such an unbalanced relationship and even if I don't completely cut them off I tend not to reply very often or take much interest in what they have to say. Obviously if they changed their minds about the "just friends" thing, then I might have more interest (but maybe not, at this stage). This puts me in control, because I'm the one that cares less. If I was continuously trying to make them like me and doing things for them, then they would be in control and they could manipulate me like a puppet. In Hong Kong women call these men "soldiers", as in "this guy is one of my soldiers. How many soldiers do you have?"

To summarise there are only two ways to leave the friend zone:

The first is to change the relationship from a friendship into something else. This is unlikely but it is possible in some cases if you do the exactly the right thing. The reason it's so unlikely is the reason you are there in the first place – you must have either done the wrong thing or not be attractive in the eyes of the other person. It's not worth banging your head against the wall here – if she doesn't find you attractive then you're never going to be "more than friends" and no technique or anything you ever say or do is going to change her mind. However, if there is at least some degree of interest and attraction then you might be able to rectify the situation by refusing to accept friendship and making your intentions clear.

The other way is to stop being friends. Although that idea might sound painful, it is actually far less painful in the long run because you will be able to move on and meet someone else. Over time, you will inevitably lose interest in this girl even though it may take many years and if she is really such a great friend then you can reconnect later in life and feel comfortable with it. Next time, don't get put in the friend zone and don't put yourself there by becoming friends with a girl that you want more with. Instead, show your interest from the beginning and if she doesn't reciprocate, move on and meet someone else.

Printed in Great Britain
by Amazon